Amigo's Blue Guitar

Sander's life is given meaning when he chooses to sponsor a Salvadoran refugee for his sociology class. He never really thinks Elias will make it to Canada, and when he does, Sander and his family must learn what it means and feels like to be a refugee, and how to best relate to someone who has endured such intense personal grief. The warmth and humour of the fully-human characters invites us to embrace the situation, be moved by it, threatened by it, and to consider how we would react.

…theatre of exceptional power…. [A] subtle, often funny and ultimately moving play.

Macleans's

*Patricia Hamilton as Martha and Guillermo Verdecchia as Elias
in the Tarragon Theatre production. Photo by Michael Cooper*

Amigo's Blue Guitar

Joan MacLeod

THE SUMMERHILL SEASON

© 1990 Joan MacLeod

The Summerhill Season is published by:
Summerhill Press Ltd., 52 Shaftesbury Avenue
Toronto, Ontario M4T 1A2

Distributed by:
University of Toronto Press, 5201 Dufferin Street
Downsview, Ontario M3H 5T8

General Editor: Michelle Maynes
Cover illustration: Dean McCallum
Author photo: Michael Cooper
Printed and bound in Canada

"Amigo's Guitar" was written by Roy Bodkin,
John D. Loudermilk and Kitty Wells
and recorded by MCA Records

Canadian Cataloguing in Publication Data

MacLeod, Joan, 1954–
Amigo's blue guitar

(The Summerhill Season)
A play.
ISBN 0-929091-34-5

I. Title. II. Series.

PS 8575.L4645A83 1990   C812'.54   C90-095779-4
PR9199.3.M244A83 1990

Enquiries regarding production rights should be directed to
Patricia Ney, Christopher Banks and Associates, 219 Dufferin Street,
Ste 305, Toronto, Ontario M6K 1Y9. Phone: (416) 530-4002
Fax: (416) 530-1848.

Running time is 1 hour and 45 minutes.

For Ninette and Rob

Amigo's Blue Guitar was first presented by the
Tarragon Theatre, Toronto on January 2, 1990
with the following cast:

ELIAS: Guillermo Verdecchia

MARTHA: Patricia Hamilton

OWEN: David Fox

CALLIE: Brooke Johnson

SANDER: Christopher Shore

Director: Dennis Foon

Set: Adam & Irena Kolodziej

Costumes: Melanie Huston

Lighting: Kevin Fraser

Sound: Keith Thomas

Stage Manager: Kate Greenway

Assistant Director: Jim Warren

Acknowledgements

This play was written with the generous
support of the Canada Council, the Banff Centre
(Playwright's Colony), the Tarragon Theatre,
and always, my family. For the dramaturgical
assistance I wish to thank Urjo Kareda, Andy
McKim, Larry Lillo, Martin Kinch and, most
importantly, the director of the first production,
Dennis Foon. I also wish to thank Guillermo
Verdecchia for his assistance with
translations. I am particularly grateful to the
friends, church workers and advocates for
refugee rights I have met since coming to
Toronto. And of course to the
refugees who told me
their stories.

Characters

ELIAS: twenty-four, Salvadoran refugee

MARTHA: sixty-five, Owen's mother

OWEN: forty-two, Sander and Callie's father

CALLIE: twenty

SANDER: nineteen, CALLIE's brother

The Setting

An island that is a short ferry ride from Vancouver. The set should have playing areas for the dock and shoreline, Elias' room and a living room/dining area of the house. The interior of the house should be simple. What dominates the set is the exterior. It contains earth, water and sky and conveys a feeling of being on the edge of an ocean.

The time is the present.

Action

Although black outs can be used, the action of the play is more or less continuous, with the end of one scene often overlapping the start of another.

Prologue

Spot up on ELIAS, *he speaks directly to the audience. Initially, his manner is very welcoming, until he makes a fist.*

ELIAS: What I sleep is my own. I am in my bed, in my room and there are no countries. There is no language to sleep. This is a true thing to all peoples. Now you are asking for the nightmare, for the dreams of me. I am not going to tell you. They are mine.

Do you see the girl in my bed? It is too dark. You must touch to see. You must see her by what you remember. I will tell you her arms, her eyes, her skin. She too would like to see the dream come out of me. This is one stupid girl.

You let the dream come out and there is no place left for me. In this house, this country. No place left inside a girl in my bed. (*makes a fist*)

This is it. This is how the dream comes out. This is the dream I will bring you.

Act One

Scene One

Interior, late afternoon, November. MARTHA *and* OWEN *enter, they have just driven up from Oregon.*

MARTHA: John Wayne looked tired. That was my first impression — give the man a rest. It should've been the happiest day of my life. How many other women look up from the breakfast dishes and see John Wayne out their window, John Wayne tying up to their dock.

OWEN: He fished up here every year. It was no big deal.

MARTHA: Speak for yourself mister. I'm running to beat the band — trying to find Sander's autograph book, braiding Callie's hair. By the time we got down there the water was calm again but he stayed on so we could all say hello. He was polite as could be. I was so mad at you Owen. Sitting up here on your duff like it was a daily occurrence. The man was a legend.

OWEN: The man was a fascist.

MARTHA: A polite legend. You were nasty just like that today.

OWEN: To who?

MARTHA: The border man. He asked if we had anything to declare and you almost took his head off.

OWEN: You know what they are Mom? Failed cops.

10

MARTHA: Don't you start with me. Carter forgave you. The whole bunch of you. Stevie Newton moved back home as soon as they granted amnesty. And Kitty's boy up in Portland? He was a draft dodger too. I never liked that expression. Draft dodger. It made you sound sneaky.

OWEN: We were. That was the point. And while we're on the subject, I'm still waiting. I didn't want a pardon. I want a goddamn apology.

CALLIE: (*enters*) You two at it already?

(CALLIE *embraces* MARTHA *and* OWEN)

OWEN: Hi sweetheart.

MARTHA: Callie. God love us you're like your mother.

CALLIE: Hi Grandma. Dad.

OWEN: You and your brother get along okay this week?

CALLIE: No. How was the drive up?

MARTHA: We stopped at Denny's near Snohomish. I had clam strips. They were tough. Are you on one of your diets Callie? You're thin.

CALLIE: No.

OWEN: Where is Sander?

CALLIE: Town.

MARTHA: What was that diet you were on the last time you were in Oregon? What was it you were eating?

CALLIE: Tab and ju-jubes.

MARTHA: Tab and ju-jubes! I thought we'd have to haul you out on a stretcher. You still seeing that guy with all the hair? Riley? Are you dating Riley?

CALLIE: No.

MARTHA: I didn't like all that hair. Did you?

CALLIE: It ruined our relationship. I'm going out with this guy that works on the ferries.

OWEN: Who?

CALLIE: Roddy Glass.

MARTHA: Is he the one who steers? We met him this afternoon.

CALLIE: Roddy parks cars. He bought his own place. You know that A-frame on Harbour Road?

OWEN: Gone five days and you found a boyfriend.

CALLIE: He's not my boyfriend. Did you see mum?

OWEN: I talked to her on the phone. I didn't do much visiting. Just went down to pick up your grandma really.

MARTHA: The Peace Arch was dirty. Did you notice that Owen? That poor old monument used to gleam in the sun.

OWEN: It looked about the same as ever to me.

MARTHA: "Children of a common mother." That's what's written up top and today you could barely see it. I always thought common meant cheap.

OWEN: I like that: a regular floozy…

MARTHA: Don't you start with me…

OWEN: I'm glad you're here.

MARTHA: Your dad wants me to stay right through the winter. He thinks I'm old.

CALLIE: We all want you to stay…

MARTHA: Meatloaf and canned corn for supper. I brought two turkeys up for Thanksgiving. Your father here wouldn't declare them.

CALLIE: We already had Thanksgiving last month.

MARTHA: Well you're having it again. This coming Thursday. Does everyone still like canned corn?

CALLIE: That's fine.

MARTHA: I don't know how to gauge the time on that old stove. Is it in the metric too?

CALLIE: Grandma it's a woodstove.

MARTHA: Well I know that. I grew up with one of those and believe you me we didn't think it was anything special. I suppose your father here will be getting rid of electricity soon so we can all ruin our eyes with a coal oil lamp. That's why your mother left. Owen wouldn't be modern. (*exits*)

CALLIE: No it wasn't.

OWEN: You tell her Cal. How were your midterms?

CALLIE: Easy. You know Dad Roddy Glass is a perfectly fine person. He's just not very good with words...

OWEN: You don't meet anyone in your classes?

CALLIE: Roddy's going to night school.

OWEN: What's he taking?

CALLIE: Air brakes. If you're so down on island guys, how come you made us grow up here?

OWEN: I could rent a place in town for you and Sander. You're spending half your day on a bus or a ferry...

CALLIE: Sander doesn't need to live near campus. He only shows up there twice a week, tops. And all he does is sit in the cafeteria . Or else he's down at immigration driving them all crazy. That's the only reason they're letting that guy come. It's so they'll have Sander off their case...

OWEN: What guy?

CALLIE: The refugee.

OWEN: I thought he died.

CALLIE: Apparently not. Immigration phoned right after you left. Sander's been unbearable Dad. He's walking around like the new Ghandi or something. Better yet he won't tell me anything. He says it's all top security.

OWEN: Where's the guy from?

CALLIE: El Salvador. Guess how much Sander knows about El Salvador?

OWEN: Give him a chance. How much do you know Cal?

CALLIE: The tallest peak is Santa Ana...

OWEN: Armed only with her major in geography Callie takes on the third world...

CALLIE: But the most famous is the volcano Izalco...

(*spot up on* ELIAS)

ELIAS: El faro del Pacifico...

CALLIE: The lighthouse of the Pacific. All of El Salvador is covered by layer upon layer of ash.

Scene Two

Spot up on ELIAS.

ELIAS: Estoy muy contento que usted me puede ver ahora. Tengo mis papeles listos si usted los quiere. (*I'm glad that you can see me now. I have my papers ready if you need them.*)

I am happy to work in Canada is good.

I like to work. My English is great.

Speak again please and slowly.

Que quiere? No entiendo lo que usted quiere y he dicho que quiero trabajar. Me gusta trabajar. (*I don't understand what you want. I want to work. I like to work.*)

No. I come to Canada to…porque…not to work solamente. I come to Canada porque…estoy inquieto. I am afraid.

I am afraid of my house. Please let me come.

Scene Three

Exterior, the next day.

SANDER: Right now I could take the 10:15 to Vancouver, Highway 99 to the States, then the I-5 all the way to Mexico then BANG! We're there — El Salvador, Guatemala. I think about that. I think about taking dad's truck and his Esso card and driving right inside those places. There are these soldiers everywhere and these Indian women making tortillas or pounding silver or something. I talk to them in Spanish and they understand exactly what it is I'm saying.

CALLIE: Did you talk to dad yet?

SANDER: No. Okay Cal. This is what you say when he arrives. Buenas dias Elias (*pronounces it as E-lie-as*). Yo soy Callie. Try it.

CALLIE: You better talk to him pretty soon.

SANDER: I will. He was already out on the boat when I got up.

CALLIE: I told him the guy might come but I never said he was going to live here.

SANDER: What's you problem? Dad will love it. C'mon. Buenas dias Elias....Yo soy...

CALLIE: Yo soy pissed off Sander! Yo soy wants to know exactly when this guy's coming, what he looks like and how long he's going to stay. Yo soy also wants to know how come we don't hear anything about this for a whole year then it's guess what?

SANDER: For your information Callie I stood in line at immigration yesterday for five hours. It was incredible: all these different languages flying around, all these very desperate people...

CALLIE: You missed your midterms.

SANDER: These very brave people. It certainly wouldn't hurt you any to spend some time down there.

CALLIE: What about your midterms?

SANDER: I didn't have any.

CALLIE: What about English.

SANDER: I dropped out.

CALLIE: Ah Christ...

SANDER: I didn't flunk out. I withdrew. Sociology too.

Christopher Shore as Sander and Brooke Johnson as Callie in the Tarragon Theatre production. Photo by Michael Cooper

CALLIE: Dad is going to go insane.

SANDER: It doesn't go on my transcript; it just says withdrawn or gone or…

CALLIE: So that's great Sander. That means you're only taking two courses. You know normal people have full-time jobs and families and a variety of hobbies and they can still do two courses.

SANDER: Well normal people are not concerned with saving other people's lives.

CALLIE: Give me a break.

SANDER: I'm on the waiting list to take industrial first aid.

CALLIE: What?

SANDER: So if I get my first aid ticket, I can work in a logging camp or even a mill. And I'll have lots of time for Elias.

CALLIE: You don't know the first thing about first aid.

SANDER: I can learn. Besides, you know what a first aid attendant does all day? Nothing.

CALLIE: What if somebody really got hurt?

SANDER: The most important thing is to not do anything. I mean I could put on Band-Aids and stuff but anything big and it's completely illegal to even touch them. And I know how to do the hug-of-life.

CALLIE: What the hell is the hug-of-life?

SANDER: The Heimlich manoeuver.

CALLIE: Well God help the guy who falls on top of his chain saw.

SANDER: Get off my case Cal. I haven't even signed up yet. I couldn't find it in the phone book.

CALLIE: And now because of some bullshit school project you've got some orphan-guy being hauled out of the jungle and forced to live with you.

SANDER: Okay, okay, okay! You know it all. I am terrible at everything. But there's one thing I do know about Callie and that's Elias. I know how I feel about him and I know I helped save someone's life — and if you think midterms or Roddy Glass or first aid mean more than that then you're absolutely stupid.

CALLIE: (*pause*) I can help. I can help you with the first aid. School too.

SANDER: I don't give a shit about school. This refugee stuff is way more important. It should be important to all of us.

CALLIE: What'd Elias do? Why'd he have to run away?

SANDER: You don't have to do anything to get nailed down there. He was a student…

CALLIE: He could stay at Roddy's place. He's got lots of room.

SANDER: Roddy Glass is practically an alcoholic.

CALLIE: No he isn't.

SANDER: When I think of Roddy, I just remember him leaning over the wharf and throwing up on some guy's speedboat. Not a terrific example for new Canadians. Stand up.

CALLIE: Why?

SANDER: Just do it.

> (SANDER *places his arms around* CALLIE *from behind and hugs her*)

CALLIE: Sander! Jesus, ow! What are you doing?

SANDER: Saving you. I rescued grandma once. Remember when
        she was practically dying over that muffin that had gone
        down the wrong way? I made it fly.

(*enter* OWEN)

OWEN: Made this crap sail right out of her like a little wet bird
      thumping against the window.

SANDER: Hi Dad. How was the trip?

(SANDER *releases* CALLIE, *embraces* OWEN)

OWEN: Good.

CALLIE: You've probably punctured my goddamned lung.

(CALLIE *exits*)

OWEN: School alright?

SANDER: Yeah.

OWEN: Cal said you did an essay on Mussolini.

SANDER: Right.

OWEN: That you copied it word for word from the junior
      worldbook.

SANDER: I changed some stuff.

OWEN: That's bullshit Sander.

SANDER: So's school. I've been busy.

OWEN: You do some work on the boat?

SANDER: Sort of.

OWEN: Sort of.

SANDER: I ran out of paint. Lives have been at stake Dad.

OWEN: Pardon me?

SANDER: You know that group I formed last year to sponsor a refugee?

OWEN: I know you left everything until the last minute and...

SANDER: Well he's coming. Elias.

OWEN: You told me he died.

SANDER: No way.

OWEN: Sander, you said he died.

SANDER: He could've been killed a million times. I said he was in danger. Grave danger.

OWEN: There is a slight difference between being dead and being in danger.

SANDER: Elias filled out the wrong forms. He said he wanted to work here and they gave him the stuff for a work visa and he got turned down. Immigration does it on purpose to slow things up because so many want in. But he reapplied and now he's coming.

OWEN: Where?

SANDER: Well here.

OWEN: To Canada.

SANDER: Right. He's just waiting in Guatemala City while they do these security checks...

OWEN: Where's he going to live Sander?

SANDER: With us. Isn't that great?

OWEN: You know what I think? That you're as organized as a two year old and you do stuff behind my back even when you don't have to.

SANDER: You're the one who's always going on about how hard it was being booted out of your own country...

OWEN: I didn't say it was a bad idea. But you've got to get organized.

SANDER: I already signed him up for English. The waiting lists are huge. Muy grande. My Spanish is really coming back.

OWEN: Where'd it go Sander? Aren't you doing Spanish this term?

SANDER: By tutuorial. How's mum?

OWEN: Actually she's going in the hospital...

SANDER: What's wrong?

OWEN: She's fine. She's getting her tubes tied. She should've done it years ago...

SANDER: Thanks a lot.

OWEN: Now this guy's gonna need some warm clothes.

SANDER: I know.

OWEN: How long will he be staying here?

SANDER: We're responsible for the first year but most refugees are on their own after three months...

OWEN: It would've been nice to have a little warning Sander.

SANDER: That's not how it works.

OWEN: If you had followed up on this properly and not forgot about...

SANDER: I never forgot him! I've written letters, stood in lines....Just because I don't announce everything I do to you and Callie doesn't mean I don't do anything. He's important to me Dad.

OWEN: Okay.

SANDER: I've thought about him every single day this year. Elias.

Scene Four

Interior, one week later.

ELIAS: Hello.

MARTHA: Why you're not a boy at all. You're a full-grown man.

ELIAS: Hon...honoured to meet you.

MARTHA: You're Elias. (*mispronounces his name E-lie-as*) Sander's on his way. He was so disappointed not to be able to go to the airport.

ELIAS: Elias, yes. Hello...

MARTHA: E-lee-as? You're sure?

ELIAS: Elias.

MARTHA: Alright, Elias it is. I'm Martha. Have you had your lunch?

ELIAS: Como....I am honoured to meet you.

MARTHA: You can call me Grandma.

ELIAS: Me Grandma.

MARTHA: CALL ME GRANDMA!

ELIAS: GRANDMA! HELLO!

MARTHA: HELLO!

ELIAS: Hello.

MARTHA: Do you like Cheez Whiz?

ELIAS: Cheez Whiz?

MARTHA: And there's enough turkey left over to feed an army.

ELIAS: (*removing carton of cigarettes from a duty free bag*) For you.

MARTHA: Oh, no. I'm not a smoker. This house is smoke-free
except for that damn stove.

ELIAS: Sugars? (*offers little packets of sugar*)

MARTHA: Isn't that nice of you. Thank you. We'll have it in our
tea. How was your trip?

ELIAS: Que? Lo puede repetir por favor? (*Can you repeat that
please?*)

MARTHA: The airplane?

ELIAS: Yes!

MARTHA: You're a long way from home. This isn't really my
home either but I guess I'm the welcome wagon. Welcome!
I've been to Mexico.

ELIAS: Mexico. Yes. I am El Salvador.

MARTHA: Just Tijuana but that was enough. We were in San
Diego; we went down for the afternoon. Reg brought the
car. Can you imagine?

ELIAS: Disculpame. Puede hablar un poco mas despacito por
favor? (*Can you speak a little slower please?*)

MARTHA: (*pause*) We were afraid to leave the car by itself. Mexico is one hot country. You'll be from a hot place too. Canada is cold but not here. It's just like home. I'm an Oregonian.

ELIAS: I...am...speaking...slowly...please.

MARTHA: You certainly are!

ELIAS: Yes.

MARTHA: Or...e...gon. I am from Oregon.

ELIAS: Como? No entiendo... (*I don't understand...*)

MARTHA: Just north of California...

ELIAS: California ! Yes!

MARTHA: Actually we're closer to the Washington end, up by Portland. Are you married?

ELIAS: Disculpame Señora pero no entiendo muy bien el ingles. (*Excuse me but my English is not very good.*)

MARTHA: Married! A wife?

ELIAS: Wife. No. No wife for me. Please.

MARTHA: But you have a family. Sisters? Brothers?

ELIAS: Two brother. Four sister.

MARTHA: You must be a Catholic.

ELIAS: Yes. Catholic. Now — no. No Catholic.

MARTHA: We're Baptist. Owen doesn't go. Sander and Callie are agnostics. Are your parents in El Salvador?

ELIAS: Parents?

MARTHA: Mother, father...

ELIAS: Mother dead. Father dead.

MARTHA: My husband's gone. He was sick a long time. Owen
came down but he couldn't go to the funeral. The FBI were
there, right in the chapel. That's sad isn't it? Having to stay
away from your own father's funeral. Him and his father
didn't see eye to eye. Reg was ashamed of him over this
draft business.

ELIAS: Do you have a birthday?

MARTHA: July the fifth. My mother went into labour during the
fireworks. You've run away too now. Like Owen.

ELIAS: Yes?

MARTHA: I'm glad he didn't go. Mabel Roderick's boy was killed
over there. Mabel hates me. She hates me because I can hop
on the Greyhound and go see my son. Viet Nam was a
dreadful business.

ELIAS: Viet Nam, yes. I am El Salvador.

MARTHA: Then everyone blamed Catherine. She was the one that
made him leave. And I kept my mouth shut but I would've
told him the same: run oh run, head for the hills everyone,
head for the hills.

ELIAS: Very bad Viet Nam.

MARTHA: Wasn't it terrible? And it split our town right down the
middle. Some people wouldn't talk to me because of Owen.
I never stopped saying hello to anyone. Cheerful too. Water
off a duck's back. The FBI used to visit me.

ELIAS: FBI...

MARTHA: Listen to me Elias! (*mispronouncing his name again*)

ELIAS: Elias.

MARTHA: Sorry, Elias. Nattering away at you and you're probably starving to death.

ELIAS: I am fine. How are you?

MARTHA: Fine! Reg bought a plaster donkey in Tijuana. It was blue. I thought he'd put it out in the garden but he kept it at the foot of our bed. Can you imagine that?

ELIAS: Como?

MARTHA: I thought it was creepy... I do! I do speak Spanish. "Amigo's Guitar." Do you know Kitty Wells?

ELIAS: How are you?

MARTHA: She's a country and western singer. The best country and western singer ever.

ELIAS: Country and western.

MARTHA: You like it?

ELIAS: No me gusta. Sorry.(*I don't like it.*)

MARTHA: I told you a fib. It did hurt me. All those people who wouldn't give me the time of day because of Owen. Berty Barnes said there was no difference between a draft dodger and a child molester or any other common criminal. It broke Reg's heart. Berty used to be one of our best friends.

ELIAS: Amigos.

MARTHA: "Amigo's Guitar" is a song by Kitty Wells and it's Spanish. Or some of it anyway. Mexican. I believe it's from south of the border.

ELIAS: Me va cantar una cancion de Mexicana? (*You're going to sing me a song from Mexico?*)

MARTHA: It'll break your heart in two if you're at all sensitive. I can tell already that you're sensitive.

ELIAS: Sing please.

MARTHA: You want me to sing? Aren't you brave.

ELIAS: Honoured...

MARTHA: Pretend my hair's black.

ELIAS: Yes.

MARTHA: Pretend I'm beautiful.

ELIAS: Usted es muy hermosa. (*You are very beautiful.*)

MARTHA: (*sings*) Tonight they're singing in the village,
>   Tomorrow you'll be gone so far,
>   Hold me close and say you love me,
>   While Amigo plays his blue guitar.
>   Aye yi, Aye yi the moon is so lonely,
>   Tomorrow you'll be gone so far...

SANDER: (*enters*) Grandma don't...

MARTHA: Ssssshhhh!

>   (*sings*) Mañana morning...

ELIAS: Mañana...

MARTHA: (*sings*) I'll be blue as Amigo's guitar.

SANDER: Hi. Yo soy Alexander.

ELIAS: I am hon...hon...

SANDER: Grandma! You made him upset. (*in dreadful Spanish*) Estoy feliz que tu estas aqui. (*I am very glad you're here.*)

MARTHA: We were only singing...

ELIAS: I am very honoured to meet you. Grandma.

Scene Five

Interior, later the same day.

OWEN: (*to* ELIAS) It's Labour Day. Catherine and I met this guy in a parking lot at Penny's. He was head of the Bellingham Cell. You've gotta remember what year it was.

CALLIE and
 SANDER: 1968.

OWEN: And I'm not kidding here, his name was Orbit Galaxy. Orbit had the distinction of being the first hippy in all of the Northwest.

CALLIE: How can you prove who was the first?

OWEN: Undisputed. Orbit was the original freak. But he had everything in order: Canadian passports, this old Valiant with BC plates. Great car. We wrecked the engine a week later but whatever... Sander?

SANDER: What?

OWEN: You're supposed to be translating.

SANDER: Mi padre tiene un amigo qui llama Orbit Galaxy. El tiene un auto como una Valiant...

OWEN: Valiant.

SANDER: El tiene Viet Nam. La guerra.

ELIAS: Si, Viet Nam.

OWEN: Because of the holiday the border is packed, which was also all part of the master plan. There's campers every-where, families on picnics at the Peace Arch. We're in line forever and Catherine's gone dead quiet. My heart is crawling up my throat but this old guy in the booth, he just asked where we were born and I said "Chilly Whack!" and he waved us through. It was a big deal.

We wanted it to be a big deal. We'd just gone over the wall, under the wire, crawled out on our bellies and arrived at a safe place. We're heroes man. The great escape. Then Catherine threw up all over her shoes not one mile into Canada and it dawns on us for the first time that she might be pregnant. She was in a hell of a mood but then she was usually in a hell of a mood no matter what....Sander!

SANDER: El paso la frontiera, no problema. Mi madre es infermo porque ella tiene mi hermana Callie.

CALLIE: What about me?

SANDER: I said you made mum sick.

OWEN: (*pause*) That's it? That's a pretty short translation.

SANDER: C'mon dad. You drove up and they waved you through. You're always making it sound like the Berlin Wall or something. Quieres dormir ahora?

ELIAS: No.

CALLIE: What'd you say?

SANDER: I asked if he wanted to go to sleep. He's had a big day.

ELIAS: Callie.

CALLIE: What?

ELIAS: Your name — Callie. Es un nombre familiar? Un apodo? De adonde viene Callie?

SANDER: Caligula.

CALLIE: What?

SANDER: He wants to know what Callie stands for...

ELIAS: Cal...ig...u..la...

CALLIE: No, no... Calico.

ELIAS: Calico. Very pretty.

CALLIE: It's ridiculous. It's a terrible name. My parents were insane. Tell him to never call me that.

SANDER: Callie. No Calico.

CALLIE: Great translating Sander.

ELIAS: Okay. Okay, Callie. Hello.

CALLIE: Hi.

OWEN: Bienvenido to soo nueva casa.

SANDER: Oh brother...

ELIAS: Thank you. Thank you very much.

OWEN: I hope you can feel at home here. I know how lonely it's going to feel at first. I hope I can help you a little with that...

SANDER: Dad...

OWEN: What's your problem Sander?

SANDER: It isn't the same. You've been pardoned. You can go back anytime.

OWEN: Well I didn't want a pardon...

OWEN and
SANDER: I want a goddamned apology.

ELIAS: Yo tengo una novia Marina. Ella se parece a Callie.

CALLIE: What's he talking about?

SANDER: I don't know.

ELIAS: Mi novia, Marina. Se parece a Callie.

CALLIE: I could learn as much Spanish as Sander knows in half an hour.

SANDER: He thinks you look like his girlfriend. Marina.

CALLIE: Marina?

ELIAS: Si.

CALLIE: Where is she now? Ask him Sander.

SANDER: Adonde esta Marina?

ELIAS: El Salvador. Hace un año que no la veo. (*I have not seen her for a year.*)

SANDER: He doesn't see her anymore.

OWEN: Man it's great. A new language. It makes the whole house feel different.

CALLIE: Ask him what he's run away from.

SANDER: No.

CALLIE: Why not?

SANDER: It's none of our business.

OWEN: And that we're sorry he had to run, that his country's in such a mess.

SANDER: He's had a long day.

OWEN: I'm very glad you're here. I'm going to bed now. Buenas noches.

ELIAS: Good night. Me too. I go.

SANDER: Tienes todos? Requerdas a donde es tu camo y el quarto de baño? (*Do you have everything? Do you remember where the bed and bathroom are?*)

ELIAS: I no understand you.

SANDER: Buenas noches.

ELIAS: Thank you. Thank you Sander. Good night Callie.

CALLIE: Elias? Are you happy to be here?

ELIAS: Happy, yes. Thank you.

(OWEN *and* ELIAS *exit*)

CALLIE: No he isn't.

SANDER: How do you know? He's just tired.

CALLIE: And sad. I thought he'd be, you know, more excited.

SANDER: He is excited. He's a warrior.

CALLIE: What?

SANDER: He's a warrior.

Scene Six

Interior, six weeks later, New Year's Eve day.
CALLIE *is wrapping* ELIAS *in bandages,* ELIAS *is studying his English books.*

ELIAS: "Where is the monkey?"

CALLIE: Hold still...

ELIAS: "The monkey is in the tree." Yeah!

CALLIE: Hold still. Make your fingers curl under. See?

ELIAS: Si. "The monkey eats the banana."

CALLIE: You're supposed to be an amputee. Your hand has been chopped off below the wrist. Comprende?

ELIAS: No I am not understanding you.

CALLIE: I'm going to wrap it. I'm going to wrap the stump.

SANDER: Gross.

CALLIE: What's this called Sander?

SANDER: What's what called?

CALLIE: This type of injury….C'mon.

SANDER: I haven't got that far in the book.

CALLIE: Saw mill accident number six.

ELIAS: You are helping me.

CALLIE: You better believe it.

SANDER: It's illegal to touch the patient.

CALLIE: What people do behind closed doors is their own business.

ELIAS: Close the door! We are closed.

SANDER: You going to give him the hug-of-life too? I'll bet Elias would like that…

ELIAS: Take off your clothes.

SANDER: Unwrap Elias. Him and me are going to a party.

ELIAS: (*verb*) Party!

CALLIE: Elias?

ELIAS: Yes Callie.

CALLIE: Have you ever killed someone?

ELIAS: Pardon me?

SANDER: Shut up Callie.

CALLIE: It's just a question.

ELIAS: No I have not. I have not killed someone. And you?

CALLIE: You know something Sander? You still have a great deal of trouble with emotional honesty. Sander and I ran into these scientologists on the Granville Mall once. They hooked us up to this machine thing called the E-Meter.

SANDER: Scientology is pure crap.

CALLIE: The E-meter measures your emotional and spiritual honesty.

ELIAS: The E-meter.

CALLIE: I, as usual, passed. Sander flunked completely. He ripped the wires right off.... So. Where's the party?

SANDER: You don't want to know where the party is...

ELIAS: My friend Roddy Glass.

CALLIE: You're going to a party at his place? Thanks a lot.

SANDER: He's working. He won't even be there.

CALLIE: Does he know there's a party at his house?

SANDER: He doesn't mind. He likes it.

CALLIE: He also has trouble with emotional honesty. When Roddy and I split up he couldn't even cry.

ELIAS: Where is the Christmas tree?

SANDER: Grandma took it down this morning.

CALLIE: If it's not down by New Years' it's bad luck.

ELIAS: I was loving the Christmas tree.

SANDER: We light it on fire.

ELIAS: Why?

CALLIE: It's tradition. A Canadian tradition.

SANDER: If you want to come tonight you can. Roddy won't be there.

CALLIE: No thank you very much.

SANDER: It's New Year's Eve.

CALLIE: No kidding.

SANDER: What'll you do?

CALLIE: I want to be alone.

SANDER: Grandma will be here.

CALLIE: I love the elderly! I don't need to get drunk and picked up and puke all night. Who'll be there?

SANDER: Everyone.

(*enter* MARTHA)

ELIAS: Hello Grandma.

MARTHA: Hello Elias.

ELIAS: Happy New Year Grandma.

MARTHA: And to you as well.

SANDER: Where's dad?

MARTHA: Walking on the beach. Owen's mad at me.

SANDER: Why?

MARTHA: He's mad I didn't breast feed him. Who likes ham?

ELIAS: I like ham.

MARTHA: Sander?

SANDER: Yes. Cal too. We all love ham.

MARTHA: Reg loved a ham supper. I'm moving to China. The old are honoured there. They wear crowns of gold and are asked advice.

CALLIE: I think that's Japan.

MARTHA: Owen just told me I should have walked into the woods to give birth. He could've fallen out on the dirt while I howled at the moon. Isn't that a terrible thing to say?

ELIAS: Yes Grandma.

CALLIE: I was born in a row boat.

SANDER: You were not.

CALLIE: I was practically born in a row boat. When mum went into labour dad was out fishing. She tried to row to the mainland all by herself.

SANDER: You were born in Lions Gate Hospital.

CALLIE: I was nearly born in a row boat.

ELIAS: I like to eat ham and eggs.

SANDER: Nearly being born somewhere is slightly different
       than…

CALLIE: I was! I was born!

Scene Seven

> *Exterior, New Year's Eve night.* CALLIE, ELIAS *and*
> SANDER *have been drinking beer for several hours.*

CALLIE: I ruined our night.

SANDER: No you didn't.

CALLIE: You know that song? "December 31st is the very worst
       day of the year…"

SANDER: It was a lousy party. This is way better.

ELIAS: Happy New Year! Trienta y una!

CALLIE: Don't tell me when it's midnight. We'll just let it slip by,
       okay?

ELIAS: Okay Callie.

CALLIE: Do you think Roddy saw me crying?

SANDER and
ELIAS: (*together*) Yeah/Si.

ELIAS: Before on this night, I am with my friends and with
       Marina. We go to one house and the other house to drink
       and all the time we are more friends. Then we go to the
       square and there are singers — Tepehuany — very good.
       We drink and sing and then we light the sky on fire.

SANDER: Fireworks. We should have bought some. We could
       light off some flares on the boat.

CALLIE: Do you miss Marina?

ELIAS: I have said good-bye and this is a long time before.

CALLIE: He changed his mind. He's going to buy a place in the Caribbean.

SANDER: Who?

CALLIE: David Bowie. He doesn't want to live here.

SANDER: No one does.

CALLIE: That's not true...

SANDER: You're always going on about all the rock stars who come here to relax, who come because it's so pretty. So we've all lived here forever and how many have we met?

CALLIE: Boz Scaggs.

SANDER: We saw him from the back. It could have been anyone...

CALLIE: It was Boz Scaggs. He owns a whole island north of here. It's common knowledge.

ELIAS: I do not know him. I do not know Boz Scaggs.

SANDER: Now Springsteen.

ELIAS: The Boss.

SANDER: I wouldn't mind having him for a neighbour...

CALLIE: Do you know why Bruce's marriage ended? She wouldn't have his child. I'd have his child in a second.

SANDER: Well maybe he'll buy a place here and you can have his baby...

CALLIE: Bruce Springsteen only lives in industrialized areas. It's common knowledge....Okay! Everybody lie back and shut their eyes...

SANDER: Christ Cal. It's freezing.

CALLIE: It's August. The sun's so hot you fall asleep in a second.
    The dock begins to drift. You sleep for hours and hours and
    when you wake up, you're in another country. A foreign
    country.

SANDER: I remember this. We used to play this all the time.

ELIAS: When you are children?

SANDER: Yeah.

ELIAS: We play these things too. We play the sand is made of
    snow and is so cold it will hurt you.

CALLIE: In this country, the men all wear dresses…

SANDER: And the ladies don't wear any clothes…

ELIAS: Take off your clothes!

CALLIE: I have to disguise myself as a boy and look after Sander
    the rest of my life. Sander'd say — tell me a better story.
    Tell me something funny that doesn't have any people.

SANDER: You always loved scaring the shit out of me…

CALLIE: We loved it, being scared.

ELIAS: (*toasting the others*) Happy New Year! Trienta y una!

SANDER: You tell'em partner.

CALLIE: Is midnight past?

SANDER: This year is officially twelve minutes old. (*to* ELIAS)
    So you had fun last year eh? That's great.

ELIAS: This was not last year. Last year I have lost this day.

CALLIE: How can you lose a day?

ELIAS: I am in a little room. There is no night and no day. I am in a prison.

SANDER: Right.

CALLIE: How'd you get out?

SANDER: You don't have to talk about it...

ELIAS: About the prison?

SANDER: Unless you want to. I mean you can if you want...

CALLIE: That's just so sad...

ELIAS: No. We are here, now. Trienta y una. Thirty One and I would like to drink with you. Sander. I would like to drink to you. I wish to thank you for bringing me here and to your house.

CALLIE: You don't have to thank him.

SANDER: You're welcome.

ELIAS: I think you must care very much for my country.

SANDER: Yeah, I do.

ELIAS: You worry with me for the trouble there.

SANDER: I think it's very important that we help. I mean there are twelve million refugees...

ELIAS: I hope one day to help you.

SANDER: I heard how five people can sponsor one. I had to do something. And even though it did cut into school and that, I think those sacrifices are essential.

ELIAS: Thank you very much Sander.

CALLIE: I can't stand this.

SANDER: This Jesuit came to my sociology classs and he gave a lecture. He was incredible.

ELIAS: Lecture?

SANDER: A talk.

ELIAS: What does he talk of.

SANDER: Well…torture. He gave a talk about the effects of torture…

CALLIE: And?

SANDER: And mercy. "Mercy occurs when those in power act with kindness and compassion." He meant us…

CALLIE: What else Sander?

SANDER: I loved that. I loved what he said about mercy and what we could do. So I did something. I mean I really did something…

CALLIE: It's March and Sander's done nothing in this course all year. He makes a deal…

SANDER: Lay off Cal…

CALLIE: Instead of writing a term paper, Sander forms a sponsoring group.

SANDER: Look Callie, I'm really sorry that Roddy Glass dumped you for the stupidest woman on the entire west coast…

CALLIE: This also means he gets to cut out of Spanish and English class and hang out at immigration. Everyone thinks he's some kind of hero plus he gets credit in three courses without doing any work.

SANDER: It was not that simple. You know it Cal…

ELIAS: (*to* SANDER) I am your homework?

SANDER: No!

ELIAS: I am the work the teacher gives you?

CALLIE: A direct quote from Sander: "It'll never happen. The guy won't ever really get here, most groups wait for years. It's all red tape and paper work."

SANDER: Fuck you. You and dad both. You can't stand it when I do anything right.

CALLIE: And all of a sudden you're a real person and you're in real danger. You have a name and a face and you're coming here. You're coming to our house. Sander isn't your saviour Elias. He was just trying to get out of writing an essay.

SANDER: Well you've written the book on saving people Callie. You've "saved" half the guys on this island.

CALLIE: It's bullshit Sander. You walking around trying to make Elias feel grateful...

SANDER: I'm not!

CALLIE: When we both know exactly why this whole thing got started.

SANDER: Who cares how it started. The point is that Elias is here and he's okay.

CALLIE: The point is you've been going around for a year thinking you're Jesus.

ELIAS: Is this true?

SANDER: I'm glad Elias has come and he's glad too.

ELIAS: I do not come because I want to. I come because I have no place to go. I am a thing for your studies? This is a funny thing. This is something I have not been before. Where is the monkey? The monkey is in the tree.

SANDER: It wasn't like that.

ELIAS: Trienta y una! Hello Canada! Do you need more help?

SANDER: You don't owe us anything...

ELIAS: No. I very much want to help you.

(ELIAS *pushes* SANDER *down*)

ELIAS: You are in this chair.

SANDER: What chair?

ELIAS: You are sitting in a chair. The chair is wood and pretty.

(ELIAS *lifts his hand suddenly as if he's about to strike* SANDER *but he refrains*)

I hit you across the face.

SANDER: What did I do?

ELIAS: I hit you again so you will tell me.

SANDER: Right. I get it. Okay.

(SANDER *tries to stand,* ELIAS *pushes him down more roughly this time*)

ELIAS: What did you do?

SANDER: I haven't done anything.

ELIAS: Bullshit! No shit! Canada is alright!

SANDER: Right....We should go in now eh?

ELIAS: What did you do?

SANDER: Nothing.

ELIAS: I hit you again.

Christopher Shore as Sander, Brooke Johnson as Callie and Guillermo Verdecchia as Elias in the Tarragon Theatre production. Photo by Michael Cooper.

CALLIE: I don't like this…

ELIAS: You are not here! I hit you again. What do you do to me?

SANDER: Noth… I, I hit you back.

ELIAS: I am much bigger than you.

SANDER: I beat the crap out of you. Now let me get up.

(ELIAS *will not let* SANDER *move*)

ELIAS: Your hands are tied behind you back. Your legs too…

CALLIE: Quit it.

ELIAS: I am now hurting every part of you. Your back, your legs, your family. Your mouth is full of blood.

SANDER: Callie!

CALLIE: Don't touch him! Don't you go near my brother!

ELIAS: You think we are stopped? I am only starting…

SANDER: (*terrified*) Oh Jesus. Don't. Please. Leave me alone!

(SANDER *frees himself from* ELIAS)

ELIAS: This is pretending.

CALLIE: Bullshit.

ELIAS: No shit! Canada is alright!

CALLIE: You're nuts…

ELIAS: I am helping Sander with his studies.

(SANDER *is stunned, still sitting, he is afraid to look at* ELIAS, CALLIE *kneels in front of him*)

CALLIE: Are you okay?

SANDER: Don't touch me, nobody touch me.

CALLIE: Look, I'm sorry…

SANDER: Just keep away.

CALLIE: Let's go home.

ELIAS: I would like this. I would like to go home.

CALLIE: He wanted to help you. It wasn't just homework…

ELIAS: I did not ask for the help of Sander.

SANDER: That isn't true.

CALLIE: (to ELIAS) Did that stuff happen? Did that stuff really happen to you?

ELIAS: Si quieres entender mi historia, aprende mi lengua. (*If you want to know my story, then you can learn my language.*)

CALLIE: What?

ELIAS: Si quieres entender mi historia, aprende mi lengua.

CALLIE: Sander? What's he talking about?

ELIAS: Quiero que pongas tu pecho en mi boca. (*I want you to put your breast in my mouth.*)

CALLIE: (to ELIAS) What are you saying to me?

(to SANDER) What's he talking about?

SANDER: I don't understand him. I don't understand either of you.

ELIAS: Si quieres entender mi historia, aprende mi lengua!

SANDER: If you want to know his story, then you can learn his language.

(SANDER *exits*, CALLIE *is very upset but she can't leave*
ELIAS, *she yells at* SANDER *who is already offstage*)

CALLIE: I'm sorry.

ELIAS: Quiero que me des tu mano… (*Place your hand in mine.*)

CALLIE: You know damn well I don't know what you're talking
about.

ELIAS: Si quieres entender lo que digo vas…

CALLIE: That isn't fair. You know how to talk to me.

ELIAS: Hablas español?

CALLIE: Yo soy… Yo soy. C'mon give me a break here. I want to
talk to you. We shouldn't have done that. Sander takes
everything too personally.

ELIAS: No entiendo. (*I don't understand*)

CALLIE: I am. Yo soy. Yo soy sorry.

ELIAS: No entiendo.

CALLIE: Yo… yo tengo?

ELIAS: Si?

CALLIE: I am sad.

(CALLIE *touches* ELIAS' *face, she runs her fingers down
his cheek as though she is tracing tears*)

CALLIE: Sad.

ELIAS: Triste.

(ELIAS *kisses* CALLIE)

CALLIE: Yo soy triste.

ELIAS: I understand. Estoy triste. I am sad now too.

Act Two

Scene One

Interior, New Year's Day, early morning. ELIAS *and* CALLIE *are in bed.*

CALLIE: Did you sleep?

ELIAS: I sleep a little.

CALLIE: I wanted to watch you sleeping.

ELIAS: Why?

CALLIE: But you were always at the window or smoking…

ELIAS: Watch me sleeping. I think I sleep like any man.

CALLIE: Can you see anything?

ELIAS: The sea.

CALLIE: Is it calm?

ELIAS: Calm?

CALLIE: Quiet.

ELIAS: Everything is quiet.

CALLIE: Does it look at all the same as down there?

ELIAS: El Salvador is very beautiful.

CALLIE: You don't think it's pretty here?

ELIAS: Oh yes but everything is very different.

CALLIE: I know what it looks like a little. I know the geology, the geography there.

ELIAS: Geografia.

CALLIE: The science of the earth's form.

ELIAS: This is the thing you study...

CALLIE: Your whole country is covered by ash. The Volcano Izalco...

ELIAS: El faro del Pacifico...

CALLIE: The lighthouse of the Pacific. We could hear the bang when Mt. St. Helens blew. Dad and Sander were out on the boat. I was afraid something had gone wrong. I love trying to imagine, you know, what's underneath these islands. When I was a kid I used to think the American border was this big red rope like in a bank line-up and when the draft dodgers were pardoned it had been let down forever. I want to learn everything. I want to know everything about you.

ELIAS: Do you have many boyfriends?

CALLIE: I went out with this guy Riley but that ended nearly a year ago now. And Roddy Glass. You know the story there. What about Marina? Does she write you or...

ELIAS: No.

CALLIE: When was the last time you saw her?

ELIAS: No te preocupas de Marina. (*Don't worry about Marina.*)

CALLIE: Did you see her after you got out of jail?

ELIAS: These are many questions.

CALLIE: How did you get out?

ELIAS: (*beat*) Avion plateado. The silver airplane is how you
make your escape.

CALLIE: Is that what you did? You and your brother took a plane
to…

ELIAS: To the mountains. Si.

CALLIE: Which mountains? I know how it looks…

ELIAS: Geografia.…And here. (ELIAS *touches* CALLIE's *face*) This is
my geography.

CALLIE: My face.

> (ELIAS *positions* CALLIE *so that she is upright and*
> *kneeling, he then uses her body as a map, he runs*
> *his hands down* CALLIE's *arms*)

My arms.

ELIAS: North America. The head, the thinking. The strong part.
This part of you is telling the other part what to do. It is
telling your legs to work…

CALLIE: Yes…

ELIAS: Here. (*kisses* CALLIE's *feet and legs*) South America. Underneath and working. Working for the top of you.

CALLIE: What are you talking about?

ELIAS: Your body. Geography. No?

CALLIE: Yes.

ELIAS: And here. (*puts his arms around* CALLIE's *hips*) Central
America. This is the asshole.

*Isabel Zatti as Callie and David Everhart as Elias in The Citadel Theatre/
Theatre Calgary production. Photo by Ed Ellis.*

CALLIE: I don't think so…

ELIAS: Everybody very happy to screw Central America.

CALLIE: No.

ELIAS: Soy un idiota. Estaba loco a noche. (*I am an idiot. I was crazy last night.*)

CALLIE: What? What is it?

ELIAS: The anger. Last night the anger comes out of me.

CALLIE: But good stuff too…

ELIAS: This will never happen again. I will make apology to your brother.

CALLIE: It's not your problem. He'll just blame everything on me….(*examines* ELIAS' *back*) The scars on your back. All the things that have happened to you…

ELIAS: Scars? No, no. They are…enfermedad, viruela…pox.

CALLIE: Chicken pox? Oh. What were you like when you were little?

ELIAS: I don't know Callie. Bad and lazy and loving to play. Just a boy.

CALLIE: Say something. Say something to me in Spanish.

ELIAS: Pienso que deberias volver a tu cuarto…

CALLIE: What? What does it mean?

ELIAS: I think you should go back to your room.

CALLIE: Why?

ELIAS: This must be kept away from your father. Your brother and grand…

CALLIE: It doesn't matter. Riley used to spend the weekends here.

ELIAS: Riley does not look like me. Riley does not live in this house.

CALLIE: You didn't want this. You didn't want this to happen.

ELIAS: I want and wanted. I wanted you. Pienso que deberias volver a tu cuarto. Good bye Callie.

CALLIE: What happened last night with you and Sander, that isn't something you should feel bad about. You can't keep everything hidden inside...

ELIAS: Go back to your room.

CALLIE: What happened between you and me isn't a bad thing either.

ELIAS: You and me. Volve a tu cuarto...

CALLIE: I don't want to.

ELIAS: Please go.

Scene Two
Interior, later the same morning.

MARTHA: Do you remember the wave after the Alaskan earthquake?

SANDER: I wasn't born. Have you seen Callie or Elias?

MARTHA: No I haven't. It put our rowboat in the rose garden and it completely demolished the town pier.

SANDER: This isn't a tidal wave Grandma. It's just a bunch of brown crud that washed up on the beach last night. Did you hear them come in?

MARTHA: Weren't you with them?

SANDER: They stayed out later.

MARTHA: Reg wouldn't move that boat back. For ten years, everyone that came to our house heard about the earth-quake, something that happened thousands of miles away that made our rowboat land in the garden...

SANDER: There's a sailboat from Seattle at the government wharf. They probably dumped something.

MARTHA: It just made me sad. Every time I'd see that silly old thing rotting out there in the bushes I'd think of all those Alaskans being swallowed up by the earth...

SANDER: Or maybe it's from a tanker...

MARTHA: I can't see anything.

SANDER: Well it's there on the shore. It looks like brown soap. An American tanker...

MARTHA: When Reg died I chopped that old boat up and put it in the trash. The past is past.

SANDER: Where's dad?

MARTHA: He went into Horseshoe Bay first thing.

SANDER: Why?

MARTHA: I don't know. Maybe he's got a girl there. Do you think?

SANDER: No.

MARTHA: I wish Owen would date more. He was seeing that Evelyn, the pot thrower, but that's nearly two years ago now.

SANDER: Evelyn was alright. I hate this. I hate never knowing where anyone is. Communication in this house is at an all time low.

MARTHA: Well. Someone woke up with a chip on their shoulder.

SANDER: I woke up clear Grandma. I'm a new man.

MARTHA: That Evelyn made me a tea pot. It had two spouts and you couldn't make a cup of tea in it for love or money. So I put it on the mantel. It's a wonder the whole mantel didn't come down.

SANDER: You should learn Spanish.

MARTHA: Why?

SANDER: So you can know what's going on. Everyone in this house should.

MARTHA: We don't have many Spaniards in Oregon.

SANDER: They're not called Spaniards, all the Spanish speaking people in this world are not Spaniards.

MARTHA: Five years ago I was in the dog house because I couldn't speak French.

CALLIE: (*enters*) Hi.

MARTHA: (*to* CALLIE) You and your little friend would come down to visit and pretend you were from Quebec City.

CALLIE: (*to* SANDER) Hi. (*pause*)

SANDER: You see the shit all over the beach?

CALLIE: Where?

SANDER: C'mon Cal it's everywhere. Open your eyes.

CALLIE: Everything looks the same as ever to me.

SANDER: Well it isn't.

CALLIE: You okay?

SANDER: Oh yeah. I'm a freak of nature; I'm happy all the time.

MARTHA: Sander's decided to start this year off contrary...

CALLIE: I know it wasn't...

SANDER: What?

CALLIE: I know it wasn't all selfish, you bringing Elias here...

SANDER: She's the one who should feel bad.

CALLIE: Grandma? What's she got to do with this?

MARTHA: I stayed in last night and watched television. I didn't whoop and holler out on the dock half the night...

SANDER: You should go right down to his room and say you're sorry.

MARTHA: Whose room?

SANDER: Elias.

CALLIE: What's with you?

MARTHA: I consider Elias to be a friend. I have certainly never had a falling out with him, never heard him get lippy...

SANDER: It's your government Grandma! Yours. They're behind everything down there. It's the Americans who are responsible for his going to jail, his being tortured, his having to run away...

CALLIE: He hasn't been...

MARTHA: Elias is my friend. And in his country, young man, grandmothers are a respected commodity.

SANDER: He should hate your guts...

MARTHA: I would no sooner cause him harm than myself or you or your sister.

SANDER: Why do you keep voting for them?

MARTHA: Whose them? Huey Angus the mayor? And we've got a Democrat in...

SANDER: I hate them. I hate Americans. They're just such liars. They're all overweight big-mouth right-wing fanatical religious nuts except they're too stupid to even know it...

CALLIE: He's mad at me. This is nothing to do with...

MARTHA: Just who do you think your mother and father are? Where do you think you come from?

CALLIE: This has nothing to do with you grandma...

MARTHA: Where do you think you come from?

SANDER: Here! I was born here!

CALLIE: I'm sorry Sander. Okay?

SANDER: I am not, repeat *not* an American!

MARTHA: You should be ashamed of yourself.

(*enter* ELIAS)

SANDER: I was born here.

ELIAS: Do not yell at the grandma.

SANDER: Don't you ever tell me what to do.

MARTHA: You owe me an apology. You should bow your head in shame. (*exits*)

CALLIE: Grandma...Jesus Christ Sander. What do you think you're doing?

ELIAS: (*to* SANDER) Buenos dias.

SANDER: It's more her fault than ours.

CALLIE: What? Is someone trying to blame someone here?

SANDER: He is. It's not my fault for saving his life.

ELIAS: Quiero hablar de lo que paso anoche. Sander? (*I wish to talk to you of last night.*)

SANDER: I don't understand you.

ELIAS: Dije que quiero hablar con...

SANDER: What?

ELIAS: Quiero...I wish to talk of last night. (*pause*) Do you wish me to go from your house?

CALLIE: No! We all just had too much beer...

ELIAS: Sander?

SANDER: Where are you going to go? This is it for you. The last stop. Like it or not, this is home.

ELIAS: Thank you very much.

CALLIE: (*to* ELIAS) Stop thanking people all the time. It's unnatural... (*to* SANDER) You made grandma cry.

ELIAS: I go to her. I go to grandma. (*exits*)

CALLIE: God, Sander. What's with you?

SANDER: Listen.

CALLIE: You're acting like a little dictator.

SANDER: Cal listen to me. I saw him last night.

CALLIE: Who?

SANDER: Elias. I saw him up close.

CALLIE: So did I.

SANDER: He put something in me. Something so sour from inside him.

CALLIE: No he didn't…

SANDER: He's full of poison.

CALLIE: Look, people who've been through stuff like he has…

SANDER: I know. Trying to help them is ridiculous. He's doomed. He was doomed way before he ever got here. And I've read about this stuff…

CALLIE: You got it all backwards Sander.

SANDER: We shouldn't have done this. I shouldn't have brought him here. People who've been tortured — it's all business as usual then all of a sudden — snap.

CALLIE: Last night he opened up, just a crack. And now you're making him pay through the teeth for it…

SANDER: I mean we hardly know anything about him or what he's been through, what he could do. How come he got out of prison? What did he do to get out?

CALLIE: The scars on his back…he says it's chicken pox.

SANDER: Right. So last night he was showing me what it was like to have chicken pox. You turned on me Callie. You made that all happen. You should keep away from him.

CALLIE: It was just fooling around…

SANDER: He scared me.

CALLIE: We can help him.

SANDER: You're crazy.

CALLIE: When I look at him it's like this chance to change the whole world.

SANDER: When I look at him I wish we'd never brought him here.

CALLIE: A chance to set things right.

SANDER: Exactly. That's what he wants, that's why he's in our house. He wants to get even.

Scene Three

Six weeks later, exterior.

ELIAS: El Salvador is not maybe going to war. It is not maybe going to war in another country. It is not the same…

OWEN: I didn't say it was the same.

ELIAS: El Salvador is at war. At war inside herself.

OWEN: Itself.

ELIAS: Hitting herself. Itself.

OWEN: I don't think you followed what I was saying…

ELIAS: I follow good.

OWEN: Get things straightened out at your English course and you'll understand a whole lot better.

ELIAS: Do not change the words for me. Continue please.

OWEN: There was just this time, this time between getting my
draft notice and coming to Canada. Everything was very
sharp, defined. Instant overview. Made the food taste better
and women...man. You put all that on top of really getting
to know women for the first time and it was incredible. You
know when the sea goes crazy? Comes right up over the
breakwater? There's something so great about that. We're
all longing to be threatened. We're all longing to be threatened again by the natural world. Cal knows that. She's very
in tune with old mother earth.

ELIAS: Yes she is...

OWEN: Sander of course used to wet the bed worrying about
earthquakes. Are you hearing anything from your people
down there? In El Salvador?

ELIAS: Some of them yes.

OWEN: And they're fine?

ELIAS: Some of them yes. Fine thank you.

OWEN: How do they feel about your having to come here? To
Canada?

ELIAS: Fine thank you.

OWEN: Did you understand my question?

ELIAS: Fine...They are sad. Grandma, she is sad too when you
leave her house.

OWEN: My mother? That's what she told you?

ELIAS: She tells you run but her heart is sad when you go...

OWEN: Well that's a long time ago now...

ELIAS: She is very good, your mother.

OWEN: I burnt my draft notice. There was this group of us, we went to Portland for the afternoon. This very big deal demonstration. It made the news. When I get home that night all my stuff has been packed up, stacked neatly by the front door. My room is bare, pictures off the wall, little league trophies cleared away. Even the bed is stripped.

ELIAS: They are helping you to leave?

OWEN: I don't exist anymore. Even the air reeks of disinfectant, they're getting rid of the stink. Not one trace. Her and the old man are eating dinner. They won't even look up from their plates. I'm asking what the hell is going on and all they give me is silence. Both of them.

Now I know damn well this is all his idea but she's not saying a word. That means she's nodding approval. It's A-okay. Turn up the juice.

ELIAS: A-okay. But your mother is a friend to you now...

OWEN: She helped out with the kids when Catherine left. It was a pretty rough time.

ELIAS: For you she goes against her husband...

OWEN: He was dead....So. Your English teacher says you're not there half the time and when you are you're asleep.

ELIAS: My English is okay.

OWEN: I couldn't give a damn whether you go or not. But if you don't go to your English class, C.E.I.C. doesn't pay. Period.

ELIAS: Canada Employment si. Que se joda la C.E.I.C. Los puercos in Manpower...I look for a job.

David Everhart as Elias, Aaron Goettel as Sander and Eric Schneider as Owen in The Citadel Theatre/Theatre Calgary production.
Photo by Ed Ellis.

OWEN: You don't have to yet....That's the point of this program:
Skills Development.

ELIAS: I have found a job for next week. I do not go back for the
English.

OWEN: Where?

ELIAS: Pizza 222-2222.

OWEN: Oh Christ...

ELIAS: I clean their house in the morning.

OWEN: Whose house?

ELIAS: Pizza 222...

OWEN: You're making a hundred dollars a week to study English. What's the rush?

ELIAS: I am an assistant-manager trainee.

OWEN: Well you can tell your manager to go screw his job and...

ELIAS: He is a good man, the manager. He is a chemist from
Somolia. I pay them back.

OWEN: Who?

ELIAS: (*producing letter from his coat*) The government,
immigration....I am in debt to them.

OWEN: (*reading*) Your plane ticket...

ELIAS: I am pay them back for the airplane. Guatemala City to
Vancouver. It is a lot of money.

OWEN: They're asking when you can start paying. You can pay
them as little as ten dollars a month if that's all you can
afford...

ELIAS: They are your friends at the C.E.I.C.?

OWEN: No, they're not my friends...

ELIAS: The man at there talks to you on his machine?

OWEN: What machine?

ELIAS: I talk to him. I have the interview and he turns on the little tape machine.

OWEN: A dictaphone...

ELIAS: Who does he talk to?

OWEN: I don't know. He's probably just, you know, making a memo to your file. Maybe telling his secretary to write a letter.

ELIAS: To who?

OWEN: It's just paper work. I wouldn't worry about it...

ELIAS: I have read the paper. They are very angry here with the refugees. Go home Tamil! Go home Iran! I have read these things. How do we go?

OWEN: Slow down. Nobody is going to make you go anywhere. Legally, whatever, they're not allowed to.

ELIAS: I have no other place to go. Eleven countries I am apply to before Canada...

(*enter* SANDER)

OWEN: I will see to it personally. You are not going to be made to leave...

ELIAS: Equador, Columbia, Panama...

OWEN: And you don't have to work until you finish English. You don't have to pay back the plane ticket until you have a job. You don't have to move from here until you're ready. You got all that?

ELIAS: Si…

OWEN: And I've got a big contract with fisheries this spring
tagging fish. You can work on the boat if you want, with us.
Right Sander? I count and mark the fish. We put this silver
tag on their fins.

ELIAS: Why?

OWEN: So we can see where they're going. It'll be good to have
another hand. Eh Sander?

SANDER: It's pretty crowded already.

OWEN: Then maybe Elias can do the first contract. You'll still
have classes then. Or exams. You should be into exams by
then.

SANDER: I'm finished.

ELIAS: You follow the fish.

OWEN: Sort of. And I pay a lot better than Pizza-Pizza.

ELIAS: You should kill the fish.

OWEN: They come down from Alaska to spawn and we keep
track of how many stay here, and how many make it down
to Juan de Fuca, to the States.

ELIAS: You wish to know the nationality of a fish.

OWEN: Right. We don't start until April so you can finish English.

SANDER: I said I'm finished school.

OWEN: What?

SANDER: I withdrew.

ELIAS: You should kill the fish.

OWEN: You've flunked out.

SANDER: I withdrew...

ELIAS: You would make more monies if you kill the fish.

OWEN: I usually kill the fish!

(ELIAS *exits*)

SANDER: It's just a W on my transcript. It doesn't mean anything.

OWEN: Oh. I'm glad it doesn't mean anything. For a while there I thought we were in serious trouble. When did this happen?

SANDER: I don't know. Two weeks ago. This first aid stuff is taking up a lot my time.

OWEN: Right.

SANDER: I'm doing okay at it. It's easier than I thought.

OWEN: Glad to hear it Sander. I wouldn't want you straining any muscles or exercising your brain...

SANDER: College. I mean it was all crap Dad. All the other students, I didn't know how to talk to anyone. They're all just pre-law, pre-business, pre-historic morons...

OWEN: Some poor son-of-a-bitch like Elias — he must be appalled by the privileges you have, the choices.

SANDER: Then let him fish the whole season.

OWEN: You bring Elias all the way up here and now you ignore him too. Withdrawn.

SANDER: I'll have my first aid ticket. You can pull your Captain Ahab routine with him.

OWEN: Fine.

SANDER: And the forest industry pays a lot better than you.

OWEN: Alright. You've got no worries then.

SANDER: That's right.

OWEN: Nothing keeping you awake at night.

SANDER: Nothing.

OWEN: What is it you care about Sander? What's important?

SANDER: Nothing.

OWEN: Whole goddamned planet's dying! What are you going to do about it Sander?

SANDER: Nothing.

(OWEN *exits, light remains on* SANDER)

Scene Four

Interior, six weeks later. CALLIE *and* ELIAS *in bed.*

CALLIE: Do you ever dream you can't speak? Maybe I'm with dad on the boat and something really terrible will happen if I can't warn him. But my throat is full of concrete. Only little noises come out, like a bird.

(SANDER'*s light goes out, exits*)

ELIAS: I do not dream.

CALLIE: That's because you never sleep...

ELIAS: And that, Callie, is because you will not let me. Always you are coming to my room.

CALLIE: Tell me not to.

ELIAS: This is a hard thing.

CALLIE: Exactly. It's snowing again. Snow in April.

ELIAS: I like the snow.

CALLIE: Coming in from the north. Maybe it will travel all the way to El Salvador. Big clouds of snow.

ELIAS: I don't think so.

CALLIE: It'll cover up the cities, the mountains…

ELIAS: We do never have snow in Salvador.

CALLIE: The layers of ash….What scares you more than anything?

ELIAS: Many things have scared me.

CALLIE: The most scared you've been, ever.

ELIAS: When I hear the knock on the door, softly…

CALLIE: Yes?

ELIAS: And there you are, back in my room.

CALLIE: I'm serious.

ELIAS: And I wish to talk of the snow.

CALLIE: Will you miss me?

ELIAS: Yes of course.

CALLIE: I miss you already. Only three more days. I wish you weren't going.

ELIAS: This is a good thing, working on your father's boat.

CALLIE: Yeah well just wait until you've been cooped up out there for a month with dad and a bunch of dead fish.

ELIAS: We do not kill the fish.

CALLIE: Dead or alive they all stink and dad's a pain in the ass.

ELIAS: And what scares you the most?

CALLIE: More than anything?

ELIAS: Yes.

CALLIE: Drunk people. People so pissed their eyes roll back in their head and you can't, you know, reason with them.

ELIAS: You have drunk people in your family?

CALLIE: No, no...just guys I've gone out with, that sort of thing.

ELIAS: Yes you do have many boyfriends.

CALLIE: No I don't.

ELIAS: Pretend the drunk man you are afraid of is under the bed or behind the door, is there in your room, always.

CALLIE: That's terrible.

ELIAS: And when you close your eyes he is there also. He never goes away, ever.

CALLIE: The people that put you in prison, they...

ELIAS: No. I am talking about a different thing. I am talking about a big fear in my country that you would not know of.

CALLIE: But I want to know. How can I understand the things that have happened to you if you won't tell me?

ELIAS: They are good things to leave behind.

CALLIE: Look at your scars. They're whiter at night, nearly silver...

Tasmin Kelsey as Callie and Guillermo Verdecchia as Elias in the Arts Club Theatre production. Photo by Glen Erikson.

ELIAS: Plateado, enfermedad, pox.

CALLIE: Bullshit.

ELIAS: No shit, Canada is alright…avion plateado.

CALLIE: The silver airplane.

ELIAS: In my prison there is an old kitchen. On the ceiling a silver wheel with a rope…una maquina… (*a machine*)

CALLIE: A winch.

ELIAS: We are take to this room to wait for the avion plateado. When the guard comes my brother's hands are put behind his back and legs and like this he is hung from the winch. Avion plateado. It is my brother that is the silver airplane…

CALLIE: But you said…

ELIAS: And the guard asks him do you wish to fly with or without a piloto…

CALLIE: A pilot.

ELIAS: Without he says. He swings my brother so hard his head is hit and hit and hit and hit into the wall and he tells him an airplane that flies without a pilot always will…choquar (makes crash sound)…

CALLIE: Crash…

ELIAS: By the time it is dark he has finished breathing. Then it is my turn. I cry that I wish to fly with a pilot. The guard laughs: "Yo soy el piloto — I am the pilot." The guard climbs onto my back. My arms break. My skins open. My eyes close.

CALLIE: (*pause*) I'm sorry.

ELIAS: This is my story. What is it you wish to do with it now?

CALLIE: To...I don't know.

ELIAS: What? This is the thing you have been wanting. No?

CALLIE: Let me hold you.

ELIAS: This is not what I wish.

CALLIE: Your other brother. Is he in danger too?

ELIAS: Everyone is in danger.

CALLIE: Let me help them or...

ELIAS: Eso es imposible.

CALLIE: Then let me help you forget.

ELIAS: This is not a true thing you are wanting.

CALLIE: I love you.

ELIAS: No Callie.

CALLIE: Yes I do.

ELIAS: You love these terrible things that I remember.

Scene Five
Interior, a couple of days later.

MARTHA: Now every spring I'd go around door to door collecting everyone's old eye glasses. The church would send them to Africa. They used to send them to the Eskimos but the Eskimos are modern now. Remember that Sander.

SANDER: The Eskimos are modern...

MARTHA: Remember to always do something extra. You should be proud of your sister. She's learned from your example.

SANDER: What'd she do?

MARTHA: She's formed a group, just like you did for Elias.

SANDER: She has?

MARTHA: Only this time it's for his brother. And she's left papers for me to sign somewhere. I'm joining her group to bring him here...

SANDER: Did you sign Dad?

OWEN: Of course I signed.

MARTHA: (*to* OWEN) Do you think your signature on something will help or hurt Callie's efforts?

OWEN: What's that supposed to mean?

MARTHA: Those terrible letters, all those terrible letters that you used to write to the draft board.

OWEN: I was expressing my world view.

MARTHA: Threatening to blow up Fort Lewis. What was the use? Writing nasty letters with no return address. Your father, Sander, in his day, was quite the character.

SANDER: I know.

MARTHA: The FBI used to visit us. Your grandfather would have a holy fit. Getting me to make tea. Reg would even offer them salmon to take home from the freezer. Now if your father stayed in college he wouldn't have been drafted, wouldn't have had to run off to Canada.

OWEN: And you'd have nothing to complain about.

MARTHA: Oh blow me up Owen! Blow up me and the Pentagon
and the whole country. I am guilty on all counts. I didn't
breast feed, I'm an American citizen, a senior…

OWEN: Nobody wants to blow you up Mom.

SANDER: And I'm not going to be drafted for withdrawing…

OWEN: Quitting.

SANDER: Withdrawing from college. You told stuff about dad to
the FBI?

MARTHA: No sir I did not.

SANDER: Good for you Grandma.

OWEN: Not the old man though. He'd have put on his old uni-
form and signed up if that's what they wanted.

MARTHA: That's not true Owen. Reg never said a word about
your whereabouts or…

OWEN: That's because he didn't know where we'd gone. I
couldn't trust him. Couldn't trust my own father.

MARTHA: Poor Sander here was eight months old before we even
knew he existed. The underground — Lord. I used to worry
Sander'd been born in a gopher hole. I'd think of you
Owen, six years old, trying to dig a hole to China in the
front yard. "Check there," I'd tell Agent Beatty. This did not
go over well with Reg or the FBI.

CALLIE: (enters) Elias back yet?

OWEN: He's still in town. He'd better not miss the last ferry. We
leave the dock tomorrow at five a.m. sharp. You sure you
don't want to change your mind Sander?

SANDER: I have an interview.

OWEN: For what?

SANDER: A job, you know, industrial first aid.

OWEN: Where?

SANDER: In this logging camp near Gold River. Just until June.

OWEN: You finished this first aid thing?

SANDER: Sort of…

OWEN: Here we go…

SANDER: I still have to do the exam.

OWEN: You didn't quit or…

SANDER: I'm doing okay.

MARTHA: Good for you Sander. Maybe you'll be a doctor one day. Or a nurse.

OWEN: So I guess you'll be going away from home then?

SANDER: It's just an interview Dad. I don't have the job or anything.

MARTHA: I could see Sander as a nurse.

CALLIE: Me too.

OWEN: I can't wait to get back to work. All this sitting around in the winter makes me crazy.

CALLIE: Dad? In two weeks, when you're around Campbell River, I might come up for the weekend.

OWEN: Why?

CALLIE: I thought the boat was family property, we're all in this together.

OWEN: You've just always hated it...

SANDER: Where're you gonna sleep?

CALLIE: With Elias. Is there any supper left?

OWEN: Pardon me?

MARTHA: You can't do that...

CALLIE: I love him.

MARTHA: I love him too honey but...

CALLIE: No Grandma, I love him. I sleep with him, you know, we make love.

SANDER: I don't believe this...

OWEN: How long has this been going on Cal?

CALLIE: I don't know. A couple of months maybe...

SANDER: Since New Year's Eve.

CALLIE: Yeah, New Year's Eve to be more specific.

SANDER: I knew it...

MARTHA: Do you know about birth control?

SANDER: Grandma...

MARTHA: It's a good question! And safety. Safety sex.

OWEN: Yeah she knows all about it.

CALLIE: What's your problem Dad?

OWEN: Did I say I have a problem?

CALLIE: How come it was no sweat when Riley stayed here. Or Evelyn or Sofie...

MARTHA: Who's Sofie?

OWEN: One thing at a time here…

CALLIE: He loves me.

OWEN: You should take it slow Cal. He comes from a whole different place, a whole other set of rules.

CALLIE: I know that.

SANDER: Maybe he'll want to fight a duel with Roddy Glass. It's very macho, Central America.

CALLIE: Shut up Sander.

SANDER: Or marry you.

CALLIE: He's been living right in the middle of a war. He hasn't exactly had a great life. You could show a little compassion Sander. All of you could.

MARTHA: I like Elias.

SANDER: I didn't know being in a war made somebody a great guy.

OWEN: Sander you're way out of line.

SANDER: I brought him here.

CALLIE: Do you want him to say thank you every day of the week?

SANDER: I want you to admit, admit it Callie, that he was a shit to me.

OWEN: What did he do?

SANDER: And you too. You set the whole thing up, you let that happen. And now you're in love. That's great. The two of you deserve each other…

Patricia Hamilton as Martha, Christopher Shore as Sander, David Fox as Owen and Brooke Johnson as Callie in the Tarragon Theatre production. Photo by Michael Cooper.

OWEN: Sander…

SANDER: You don't know anything about it Dad.

OWEN: I have some sort of idea of how he might be feeling.

MARTHA: When your grandfather came home from the war…

OWEN: Oh Jesus. Here we go…

MARTHA: You listen to me Owen. Your father, (*pause*) he had seen, he had participated in some things that I believe were unspeakable. Terrible things.

OWEN: Why would someone who'd been through such awful things be so anxious for their kid to go through the same thing?

MARTHA: Maybe it was a way of letting you in…

OWEN: I would walk through hell for Sander. If I thought someone was going to harm him or hurt him in anyway. That is slightly different than getting Sander to walk through hell for me.

CALLIE: (*pause*) Did grandpa talk to you about the war? About all that stuff?

MARTHA: No. But you'd know he was thinking about it, even years later when he was home safe and sound.

CALLIE: How?

MARTHA: Well he'd do odd things.

SANDER: Elias does odd things.

MARTHA: He'd finally get around to filling in the potholes on the driveway but it would be four in the morning and raining. There he'd be. Out there in his pyjamas and overcoat, digging and grading in the black of night.

CALLIE: You wouldn't ask him about it?

MARTHA: You can't get inside someone's skin Callie. I think I tried to do that when we were first married. But those things were, well, they were his. People don't always work things out. Young people don't know that. Isn't that strange? Young people don't know that at all....I want to sign the form to help Elias' brother. I want to help.

CALLIE: It's here.

SANDER: Grandma can't sign. You've got to be a Canadian citizen or landed.

MARTHA: Landed! I'm landed. What on earth is that supposed to mean?

OWEN: You're still in orbit Mom. Same old track, round and round.

MARTHA: Well I can give some money.

OWEN: (to SANDER) Are you going to sign?

SANDER: No.

OWEN: No?

CALLIE: What an asshole Sander...

SANDER: You're all so phoney about him.

CALLIE: I love him.

SANDER: He's taking money from grandma, he took my job on the boat and now he's screwing Callie and that's all just fine. It's all so phoney.

CALLIE: It is not screwing...

SANDER: You invent stuff. He's just another foreign guy in a ski jacket. He wants a big car and...

OWEN: (*handing him the envelope*) Read this. Try remembering all the reasons you brought Elias here in the first place.

SANDER: I know all about sponsorship. I know how good you feel when you're filling out the goddamn forms. I also know it was the most dumbfuck thing I ever did in my life.

MARTHA: Sander!

OWEN: Read Callie's reasons for bringing his brother here. They're good.

SANDER: I tried to be a friend to him. He hasn't been fair to me.

OWEN: This isn't about making friends. It's about saving lives.

SANDER: It's sealed.

CALLIE: It can't be. Elias hasn't filled out his part yet.

SANDER: (*opens envelope and reads*) Yes he has.

MARTHA: Elias is kind. I would consider it a privilege to help his family.

CALLIE: Thanks Grandma.

SANDER: How come Elias' brother has a different last name than him?

CALLIE: He doesn't.

SANDER: And his first name's Marina.

OWEN: Marina?

MARTHA: Who's that?

SANDER: He wants to bring her here. He wants to bring his real girlfriend here behind everyone's back.

CALLIE: Marina.

Scene Six

Interior, a couple of hours later. SANDER *has been waiting up for* ELIAS *in* ELIAS' *room.*

ELIAS: Hola Sander.

SANDER: Hola fuckhead.

ELIAS: Fuckhead? Okay fuckhead hello. I am at Park Royal. I have bought rubber boots for the fishing.

SANDER: Gumboots.

ELIAS: Gumboots?

SANDER: Any word from Marina?

ELIAS: Marina…

SANDER: Marina Martinez?

ELIAS: Tienes noticias de Marina? (*There is word of Marina?*)

SANDER: How stupid do you think we are? Did you think she'd just walk off the plane one day and grandma would set an extra place for supper?

ELIAS: Please tell me if you have heard from Marina.

SANDER: I mean lying like that.

ELIAS: I don't understand…

SANDER: You're a liar!

(SANDER *pushes* ELIAS)

ELIAS: When I leave Salvador my leaving puts Marina in an even bigger danger. Please…

SANDER: And Callie's got feelings too you know. You hurt her.

ELIAS: I am sorry. I do not mean to make a hurt to Callie.

SANDER: When mum left Cal kept weapons in her bed. A rock, a stick, this old umbrella. No one was ever going to hurt her.

ELIAS: But if you have heard of news of Marina I am asking you to tell me please!

SANDER: Cal hasn't even filed the sponsorship yet. It'll take years.

ELIAS: Years...

SANDER: You know that. I knew who you were way over a year ago. I knew your name. There's this office in a church in Vancouver. A cardboard box full of files. All these names, all the people in danger. I chose you. I chose your name.

ELIAS: Why my name Elias?

SANDER: Your name (*beat*) talked to me. I invented the place you were from: this little village in the mountains. I'd try to imagine your day and...

ELIAS: San Salvador is big like Vancouver.

SANDER: I wished something good for you every morning. First thing. I'd wish for your safety and then I'd wish something so you wouldn't give up hoping. Maybe something that tasted good. Maybe a good dream. Something that would keep you going. It was the best thing I ever did. You turned on me. You tried to put your hate inside me. You lied to me, you lied to my family. That name in the box turned on me.

ELIAS: Venenos. Venenos adentro de mi.

SANDER: English.

ELIAS: Poison, bad stories live inside me. I try. I am try very hard to not let the bad dream go outside me.

SANDER: This whole thing just got so messed up…

ELIAS: The name in the box in the church. The name is now Marina. Make the name talk to you. The name goes into you and you will wish her one good thing everyday. Do you like her name? If you do not like her name there are also the names of others. Miguel, Alberto, Theresa, Juan…You do not have to pretend the place they live. I can tell you these things. Sander? Marina is small. She comes from the north. Let me tell you her house. Marina. Let her name talk to you. Let me tell you her voice, her hair, her eyes, her skin…

(SANDER *comforts* ELIAS)

Scene Seven

Exterior, six weeks later.

MARTHA: (*sings*) They've hushed the singing in the village,
All is quiet beneath the stars,
Amigo sings Hasta Luega…

(CALLIE *comes up under* MARTHA)

CALLIE: Gabriola, Cortes, Galiano, Valdez…

MARTHA: Upon his lonely blue guitar.

CALLIE: I always thought the names were fancier than the islands themselves. Very lady-like.

MARTHA: What names?

CALLIE: Saturna, Texada...the names of these islands. Like a piece of lace dropped over the same old rocks and trees.

MARTHA: *(referring to envelope at* CALLIE's *feet)* What's this Cal? Is there news?

CALLIE: I don't know.

MARTHA: You haven't even opened it.

CALLIE: Sander and I used to think all the islands went all the way to the south pole....None of the Spanish explorers stuck around here. Why do you suppose that was?

MARTHA: You owe it to Elias. He'll be anxious for any word...

CALLIE: I don't owe him anything.

MARTHA: And they're still out fishing for another week...

CALLIE: I tried Grandma. I wanted to listen.

MARTHA: I know sweetheart.

CALLIE: He wouldn't trust me. He can't trust anyone. And it's only been a month since I filed the sponsorship. It takes immigration a month to answer the phone. Central America is made up of a series of shifting plates. Did you know that?

MARTHA: Well I don't think immigration would write to you just for the fun of it.

CALLIE: No wonder it's so screwed up. They're all walking on eggshells. You open it...

(MARTHA *opens the letter and reads)*

Sander thought that once we were big enough we could walk and row and sail and follow the islands all the way to South America. He wanted to visit the people that lived underneath the world...

MARTHA: "The proposed sponsorship of Marina Martinez has been declined."

CALLIE: She can't come? Why?

MARTHA: They can't find her. Well maybe no news is good news.

CALLIE: I don't think so...

MARTHA: You try again then Callie or phone them. Maybe you filled out her name wrong or...

CALLIE: I never meant her any harm. We better get in touch with the boat, with Elias.

MARTHA: People don't just disappear.

CALLIE: Yes Grandma, they do.

> (*light remains on* CALLIE *and* MARTHA, *another light comes up on* ELIAS, *he is kneeling before his empty bed*)

Epilogue

ELIAS: What I sleep is my own.

I am in my bed, in my room and there are no countries.

There is no language to sleep.

This is a true thing to all peoples.

Do you see the girl in my bed?

It is too dark. You must touch to see her.

Her arms break, her eyes close.

She is gone. Desaparecido, disappeared.

Do you want it?

Do you have a place to put her story?

(MARTHA comforts CALLIE)

MARTHA: Oh mercy. Oh mercy me.

The end

The Invention of Poetry

Paul Quarrington

Once upon a time Gary pitched in the majors.
He even has a bubble gum card to prove it.
Moon was once nominated for the Nobel Prize
for his poetry, but that was years ago. Now they
both live and drink in their hideout from the
world, a fleabag hotel. Tonight the plan is to
stay sober and to create a poem of beauty and a
joy forever. But writing poetry
requires a muse…

Paul Quarrington has won several awards for
his writing including The Stephen Leacock
Memorial Award for Humour for *King Leary* in
1987, and the Governor General's Award for
Whale Music in 1989.

Memories of You

Wendy Lill

The life of Elizabeth Smart pivoted on a
turbulent affair that produced one book and
four children. When her youngest daughter, the
resentful and drug-ridden Rose comes to visit,
an explosion of emotion between mother and
daughter erupts, as well as an explosion of
memories for Smart.

*Memories is beautifully written... Everything about
it reaches for the ecstatic — its pleasure, its
sensuality and its pain. Memories is a courageous
and profoundly moving play...*

ROBERT ENRIGHT, CBC RADIO

Fire

Paul Ledoux and David Young

Inspired by the lives of cousins Jerry Lee Lewis and Jimmy Lee Swaggart, *Fire* tells the story of two Razorback, Arkansas brothers who follow different branches of the same road of pride, lust, and greed. Cale sells his soul to rock and roll, Herchel to TV evangelism. Both love Molly, who loves both of them. *Fire* ignites with the passion of love, Jesus, and the music of rock 'n roll and gospel.

This show has drawn large audiences because the story is so powerful and so plausible... Fire is a dynamic piece of theatre...

THE GLOBE AND MAIL

Midnight Madness

Dave Carley

Wesley and Anna haven't seen each other since they both quit high school years ago. Their reasons for quitting were as different as they were, or so it might seem, until they discover plenty they never knew about each other in the bed department of Bloom's furniture store.

"A gentle little comedy…a play that will delight and touch audiences for years to come."

TORONTO STAR